Alex Gail

The Help to Buy Scam: A scheme to exploit young people and prop up a vulnerable market

Alex Gail

www.HelpToBuyScam.com

Part of the series Defeating the Poverty Ladder

© 2016

Published by Digitulip

About this book
    4
Quote
    6
Introduction
    7
Chapter One - Helping you to pay more
    9
Chapter Two - Winners and losers
    14
Chapter Three - Help to Save (the market)
    19
Chapter Four - The scam must go on
    24
Chapter Five - Help!
    29
Chapter Six - After Sales: Damage Limitation
    35
Conclusion
    39

ABOUT THIS BOOK

About this book

This book is aimed primarily at young individuals, couples and families in Britain, who—with the best of intentions—are on the verge of putting their trust in the government's *Help to Buy* scheme. Taking just a few hours to digest the arguments in this book could help you immensely to understand how the scheme works and, crucially, how the scheme works against you.

The trappings of excessive debt taken on at inflated property prices are exposed throughout this book and serve as useful reading to people of all ages and in all parts of the world. History has shown how people can engage in reckless behaviour, against their own rational interest, when following a herd mentality. The pursuit of ever-rising house prices is one example of such recklessness.

At the risk of disappointing readers hoping for great

conspiracies to be revealed in this book, the explanations for the current state of affairs are largely to be found in demographics, voting patterns and poorly-aligned interests.

Hopefully, our arguments will convince you to give *Help to Buy* a wide berth and to think differently about buying a home in general—potentially saving you huge amounts of money and stress over the next few decades.

"Man errs as long as he doth strive."

"Es irrt der Mensch, solang er strebt"

—J.W. von Göthe, *Faust / A Tragedy* (1808)

INTRODUCTION

In these early decades of the Twenty-First century, what was once an aspiration for many—buying one's own home—has become an unassailable goal of modern life. We call this great mission, pursued by millions at almost any cost, quite simply, *"the Dream"*.

The Dream is particularly prevalent in Britain, but it is also keeping young people awake at night in other parts of the world, especially, one should note, in other English-speaking countries, such as Ireland, the United States, Canada, Australia and New Zealand. No doubt it is something to do with our common language (the emotive term *"Property Ladder"* springs to mind, which doesn't appear to exist in other languages).

In these parts of the world in particular, property ownership has morphed from aspiration to obsession, from ambition to religion. In this series of books (*Defeating the Poverty Ladder*) we address this dangerously dogmatic approach to home ownership and we propose actionable solutions so that readers may avoid its most disastrous consequences, particularly for the younger generations (generations Y and Z, born since 1980), who find buying a home obnoxiously unaffordable.

In 2013 the British government came up with a grand plan, in several phases, in order to "help young people get that first foot on the Property Ladder", branded *Help to Buy*. Within the context of *the Dream*, the stated objective of this scheme was never likely to face any public resistance. After all, how could you possibly object to the people's right to own their own home?

What sounded like a nice idea on the surface was built, however, at best on economic illiteracy, at worst on intellectual dishonesty. A *Help to Buy* scam? Let's unravel this whole charade.

CHAPTER ONE
Helping you to pay more

The narrative behind *Help to Buy* goes as follows: Although mortgage rates are at record lows and monthly repayments should logically be affordable, young people often cannot buy their first home because they struggle to afford the required deposit. A deposit of 20% on an averagely priced £300,000 home is beyond the reach of most first-time buyers. Indeed, when you're 30 years old, still saddled with student debt and trying to start your career in a credit-crunched jobs market, it is unlikely that you will have £60,000 burning a hole in your pocket.

Mortgage lenders are often unwilling to offer mortgages worth more than 80% of the property value, quite simply *because* they know how vulnerable the market is to a 10%+ fall. Your bank of course has absolutely no desire to lose any money in the transaction, so they charge a lot more for taking this risk. Or they don't take the risk at all. Maybe this unwillingness alone should be sufficient to send alarm bells ringing.

But don't listen to the alarm bells for the time being.

Illustration: A £15,000 deposit without and with *Help to Buy*

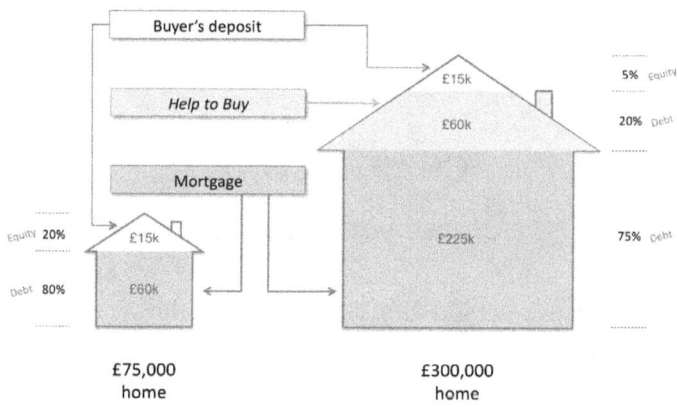

Let's imagine a realistic scenario where you can only stretch to £15,000 for your deposit, whether from your own savings or from the Bank of Mum & Dad. (Sorry, people without wealthy parents.)

What if the government simply lent you the remaining £45,000? Or, perhaps they could encourage your mortgage lender, via a government guarantee, to increase their loan from 80% to 95%?

Both would have the same effect—namely, to boost your spending power considerably. The government currently offer you both options under *Help to Buy*—an

The Help to Buy Scam

"equity loan" or a mortgage guarantee[1]—; choose your poison.

Let's choose the first option in this example and take advantage of the full 20% that the government are willing to offer—that's an extra £60,000 of spending power thanks to *Help to Buy*. (It even increases to 40% in London.)

The so-called "Help to Buy: equity loan" sounds like a great solution: Now, in addition to a £225,000 mortgage (75% of £300k) you are borrowing £60,000 (20%) from the government, so that's £285,000 (95%) in total. You can then start to pay this mortgage back, on a monthly basis, at relatively low interest rates for the time being[2]. (Alarm bells, anyone?) You only need to find £15,000 of your own in order to buy the house. It sounds like you just got richer overnight—help to buy indeed!

This doesn't make you any better off, by the way; what is happening is straightforward: The government are saddling you with even more debt. With or without the government's so-called help, your equity in your new home (i.e. what you don't owe anyone else) is the original £15,000 that you scraped together. No more, no less.

It makes no difference that the government call it an "equity loan"; it's not equity at all, it's debt!

It is essentially interest-free for the first five years, after which interest—a "fee"—of 1.75% kicks in (and subsequently rises). An "equity loan" with a "fee"... Why not simply call it debt with interest? Given how confused most first-time buyers already feel by the process of buying a home, this is a shameful use of language on behalf of the *Help to Buy* scheme, deliberately designed—we suspect—to mislead you. Equity is what you own, not what somebody else lends you. The difference here versus a conventional loan is that the government have a claim to a *percentage* of the property's resale value (in this case 20%)—whereas a mortgage loan entitles your mortgage lender to a claim to a *fixed amount* (in this case £225,000). In either case, you must pay the money back at some point.

An accountant would tell you that by taking the government's so-called help, your assets have increased by £60,000, but so have your liabilities. You own a house with greater value but you owe more money against it. You are neither richer, nor poorer (for now); you are simply more "leveraged", i.e. more exposed to the risk of price swings[3].

Your only victory by signing the government's devil pact is that you get to fulfill *the Dream*. You can be the judge of that victory later.

Whereas you *should* (in a financial sense) be able to afford a paltry £75,000 for a home without government assistance (equal to your £15k deposit plus an 80% mortgage of £60k), you are now magically able to pay £300,000 for it.

Let's look at this from the seller's perspective. Without *Help to Buy*, Mrs Smith, hoping to sell for £300,000, might have had to settle for a price of £280,000 from another buyer—let's imagine a young couple, who are not exactly wealthy but have more equity than you. Yet she is now able to sell the house for £300,000. You just made her day; thank you very much.

Based on this transaction, the seller is objectively

The Help to Buy Scam

£20,000 better off thanks to you. In other words, the government fueled a mini bidding war between you and the other potential buyer, in which the declared winner is you (the first-time buyer) but the actual winner is Mrs Smith, who was able to sell her house at a higher price than if the government had not intervened.

So in any factual sense, it is fair to call it a *Help to Sell* scheme.

CHAPTER TWO

Winners and losers

> You may be familiar with the upbeat message that eBay send you when you are the highest bidder in a particularly fierce auction: "Congratulations, you won the auction!" they tell you.
>
> "Winning" an auction means of course that you were prepared to pay more for the item than anyone else; whether this is a genuine victory or not may take time to reveal itself. Are you the sucker who overpaid the most? Perhaps you were the shrewdest assessor of value?
>
> In all bidding wars however there is a clear winner: the seller.

Whilst some may feel that you are simply fulfilling your

The Help to Buy Scam

God-given right to own your first home, it is worth noting that the young couple from the previous chapter who "lost" the bidding war to you—despite being wealthier than you but without access to *Help to Buy*—are now the ones priced out of *the Dream*. The number of young people actually getting access to home ownership is no greater; only the price is higher.

What *should* have happened (again in a financial sense) without government assistance is that you would have simply lost the bidding war (and most likely "won the game" in a wider sense). The other interested buyer would have "won" the auction, perhaps paying £280,000 for the house, but not £300,000. So without *Help to Buy* there to help the seller to sell, the seller is of course worse off.

Looking at the market as a whole, British property prices would almost certainly be significantly lower than they are without the help of *Help to Buy* since 2013.

This is just basic supply and demand. When the supply of homes is capped, any help or subsidy or encouragement to the demand side of the equation simply serves to drive up prices. As we should all know, the only two ways to bring about a fall in market prices are (a) to increase supply or (b) to reduce demand.

Of course, the government's narrative also includes the farcical idea that by stimulating demand via *Help to Buy*, housing developers would be more inclined to build additional homes, safe in the knowledge that the demand is there. But this is utter nonsense. The main obstacle to building more homes was, and still is, a lack of available land to build on.

Graph: Falling interest rates since the late 1970's

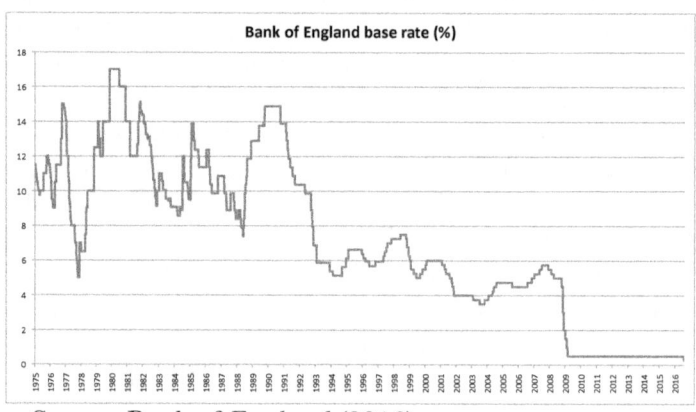

Source: Bank of England (2016)

There is another dimension to the flawed notion that many young people can afford the monthly repayments, but not the deposit. High prices don't just spring out of nowhere; prices are high *because* the monthly interest repayments are relatively affordable. Interest rates across the world have generally been on a steady downward path since the late 1970's and are currently held fractionally above zero by the major central banks. Interest rates essentially cannot fall any further than current levels. If and when interest rates rise again, it will become harder for mortgage borrowers to afford their monthly repayments and, inevitably, property prices will decline. This means that a young person who just recently bought a house at an inflated price would suffer the double whammy of higher monthly repayments, *plus* a fall in the value of their investment.

Just to make that point crystal-clear: Buying an overpriced home today with *Help to Buy* entails the realistic chance that in a couple of years, your monthly payments will increase, whilst at the same time your entire investment (and more) will get wiped out as you fall into negative equity. Double whammy indeed.

Falling into negative equity isn't necessarily a calamity if it is short-lived and if you can be patient. But what if you don't have that luxury? (We cover this in more detail shortly.)

Even the Governor of the Bank of England at the time, Sir Mervyn King, criticized the *Help to Buy* scheme as soon as it was announced, not least because of the baffling amateurism of the plan's underlying economics.

Projects are often blamed for the fact that they work "in theory, but not in practice"; *Help to Buy* doesn't even work in theory. Economists also suspected, as many observers still do, that the government's motives lay elsewhere than with genuine assistance to aspiring first-time buyers.

A crucial point: As we shall explore shortly, the UK government, and particularly the Conservative party, *have a vested interest in ever-rising house prices*. It doesn't take a huge leap of imagination from here in order to see why ministers would bake up such a dangerous scheme. Namely a fantasy scheme that *claims* to benefit everyone, especially first-time buyers, but which in theory and in reality benefits only sellers, whilst deliberately *penalising* first-time buyers.

The fact that existing owners of absurdly overpriced

Alex Gail

English homes constitute the core electoral base of the government should come as no surprise to anyone not familiar with British politics. Conversely, the fact that young people have a tendency to not vote at all also serves to explain why they so often get a raw deal. Frankly, you are being scammed.

CHAPTER THREE

Help to Save (the market)

Queen: Yes, but wait till you taste one, dearie. Like to try one, hm? Go on. Go on, have a bite. And because you've been so good to poor old Granny, I'll share a secret with you. This is no ordinary apple, it's a magic wishing apple.
Snow White: A wishing apple?
Queen: Yes! One bite, and all your dreams will come true.
Snow White: Really?
Queen: Yes, girlie. Now, make a wish,

and take a bite.
Snow White: Oh, I feel strange.
[Starts gasping for air]
Queen: [to herself] Her breath will still. Her blood congeal.
[Snow White drops onto the floor]
Queen: [Cackling] Now I'll be fairest in the land!

—Snow White and the Seven Dwarfs (1937)

Probably the least harmful weapon in the *Help to Buy* arsenal—at least on the surface—is its most recent offering, the *Help to Buy: ISA* (Individual Savings Account). As savings products go, it is incredibly generous: Pay upto £200 per month into a savings account and, at the point in time when you wish to buy a home, the government will top up your savings with a delicious 25% bonus. Based on £24,000 saved over five years (the maximum that a couple can save under the scheme), the government will give you an additional £6,000 to put towards your deposit.

And that is the crux of the *Help to Buy ISA*: You will only receive your "government bonus" if and when you buy a home. You have to be a first-time buyer and the purchase price cannot exceed £250,000 (or £450,000 in London).

The Help to Buy Scam

You also have to purchase the property with a mortgage, even though there is no clarity as to how large that mortgage need be. (Perhaps wealthy buyers could ask their bank for a minuscule mortgage, which they pay off in one easy monthly payment.)

Furthermore, you are not allowed to rent the property out; it is intended for your primary residence only. That said, according to the official *Help to Buy* website (www.helptobuy.gov.uk), "the Government recognises that your personal or professional circumstance may change at some point in the future, in which case you may need to rent out your property". It is difficult to see quite how this would be enforced. (What if these circumstances were to change just one week after moving in? And what if you chose to rent out your property on Airbnb "from time to time"?)

For all the scheme's loopholes and somewhat arbitrary conditions, the main benefit of the ISA bonus is that so long as you fulfill the conditions, your savings earn an extra 25% in hard cash from the government—with no strings attached. This extra cash is genuine, bona fide equity that you can put towards your new home.

So from your perspective, taking nothing else into consideration, it is a pretty good deal. And even if you decide, after saving up for five years, not to buy a house after all (thereby foregoing the bonus), you still have access to all the money you saved, with interest. Indeed it sounds like a free lunch with nothing to lose.

There are nevertheless a few glaring objections. (The alarm bells are back.)

First of all, the government can only pay Paul by

robbing Peter, in the form of taxation. Needless to say, the *Help to Buy: ISA* is a direct example of using the UK taxpayer in order to prop up the housing market, whereby the government are (quite literally) giving buyers at the bottom of the market greater spending power.

Naturally, the government will claim that they are "helping hard-working families" through this scheme. But hard-working families also bear the brunt of rises in taxation. To redistribute wealth in this way implies that house prices deserve to be subsidised, whereas paid work and consumer spending—via income tax and VAT— deserve to be taxed. Hard-working families who don't take advantage of this scheme therefore have to work a little harder each year in order for others to receive their government bonus.

The second major objection to the *Help to Buy: ISA* is that, although it is free money in your pocket, it is still quite small-fry in the grand scheme of things. If you and your partner have saved up 5% of the £250,000 required to buy a home—that's £12,500—, the government will hand you a bonus of £3,125. Nice to have, but your total deposit of £15,625 still represents just 6.25% of the purchase price. Which means that you would still need to take out a whopping 93.75% mortgage in order to afford to buy the home—more than most banks will lend you. Most likely then, you will have no choice but to subscribe to one of the other, scammy, *Help to Buy* schemes, such as the "equity loan".

And what is the likelihood that you would be able to resist getting sucked in? Faced with the alternative of "losing" the government bonus if you chose not to buy a home after all with the deposit you have saved, it would take a colossal amount of self-restraint, perhaps even masochism, in order to turn down this juicy pile of free money. "Use it or lose it", the government are telling you in no uncertain terms with regards to the bonus.

But as with an apple offered by an evil queen, it is often wise to turn down a free lunch. Navigating the choppy seas of the property market for the first time is challenging enough. The last thing you need is a siren like the *Help to Buy: ISA* calling on unsuspecting young buyers and drawing them closer to the rocks.

CHAPTER FOUR
The scam must go on

Or could it be that young people will in fact be saved by another government scheme, called the *Starter Home Initiative*, which promises young first-time buyers a 20% discount off the market price of a so-called "Starter Home"? Here is the government's emotive press release from February 2015 (three months before a general election):

> The move is the latest major push from the government to get Britain building and help hardworking young people secure the dream of home ownership with potential discounts of around £100k per house.

The Help to Buy Scam

With average house prices for first time buyers in England standing at around £218,000, a new Starter Home could save young first time buyers across the country an average of £43,000-helping to get them onto the housing ladder.

The plans will allow young first time buyers the opportunity to secure a new Starter Home at a 20% discount to the market price.

The properties will also have to remain available at 20 per cent below market value for the first five years – meaning any first-time buyer who looks to resell within the first five years will have to offer this discount to the next first time buyer.

Source: www.gov.uk/government/news/young-first-time-buyers-can-register-online-for-100000-cut-price-homes

The mere use of such terms as "help hardworking young people secure the dream", "get them onto the housing ladder", "opportunity to secure a new Starter Home" are red flags suggesting that this is a less-than-perfectly objective and economically sound proposal. It is indeed mostly propaganda in the run-up to an election.

First of all, who defines the market price? Perhaps the seller (a house builder), with the local council's approval, will simply define the "market price" 25% higher than what was originally planned. Instead of applying a 20% discount to a price of £300,000, why not start with a made-up "market price" of £375,000?

By applying the 20% discount to £375,000, we magically get back to a "discounted price" of £300,000—back to where we started. So far so cynical, but this is just rational behaviour on behalf of the seller.

However, let's give them the benefit of the doubt for a second. Even if house builders were indeed tripping over each other to offer buyers 20% discounts on these new starter homes versus the market price, then these buyers would naturally expect similar discounts from existing "starter homes". This is simply due to normal competitive forces: If existing starter homes are being offered for £300,000 but the new ones cost £240,000, why should you be willing to pay any more than £240,000 for an existing house? You are a rational buyer, after all.

The repercussions would be calamitous: This means that existing home owners have to take a 20% hit to their starter house prices, because of this parallel market, most likely driving them into negative equity. In this *Starter Home Initiative*, it appears, it is the first-time buyers of yesteryear who are being screwed over.

In the end, our fears may have been overblown. This

The Help to Buy Scam

particular initiative appears to have been shelved following the 2015 election, even though the disturbingly inelegant website dedicated to the scheme remains online for now (www.new-homes.co.uk/starter-homes/). But it serves to illustrate just how willing the government is to concoct poorly thought-out schemes, simply in order to give the impression that it is on the side of young aspiring buyers.

It should be clear by now what the heart of the problem is. Recall what we covered earlier regarding supply and demand. Whenever lawmakers attempt to address a supply-side problem (a shortage of homes) with a demand-side policy ("helping" buyers), you should be deeply suspicious and keep your distance.

The language they use is simple window-dressing in order to cover up what is truly at stake in a property market bubble: Too many people are holding too much property debt and too large a share of their pension wealth is tied up in housing. Yet by any measure of historical affordability, prices need to come down drastically. It is a ticking time bomb, threatening to break the banks and crush the economy, but it is too late to reverse course.

Instead, excessive and continually-rising property valuations allow the debt mountain to be considered "sustainable" for a little bit longer—a modern technique known as "Extend and Pretend". But once price rises do slow and, even worse, head into reverse, millions of households throughout the UK and beyond—young households especially—will be plunged into negative equity, left with huge debts that vastly outweigh the value of their assets. This has already happened in Spain,

Ireland, the United States and elsewhere since 2008. Displayed in every estate agent's window should be the public health warning, "Prices do not always go up".

But because for the most part, older generations (who vote) already own homes, but younger generations (who vote less) are struggling to buy homes, there is a cruelly effective trick at play: Let us sell the younger generations even harder on *the Dream* of home ownership, whilst simultaneously promoting irresponsible policies that saddle them with more debt, so that they may continue to drive prices higher for everyone else. If a day of reckoning is due, then at least let us delay it for as long as possible.

CHAPTER FIVE
Help!

So what is a young person of Generation Y to do, faced with the unattractive choice between buying with *Help to Buy* and not buying their first home? We see three angles, but ultimately only one solution.

If you subscribe to the delusion that you simply *must* own a home, at any cost, in order to qualify as a fully-fledged adult, then most likely your willpower will eventually cave in and your emotions will get the better of you. Sadly, you stand as a prime candidate to get sucked into *Help to Buy* or whatever the next "buyer abuse scheme" might be. You will probably do so with the full blessing of your bank manager and of your family, particularly of the older generations, and with a sense that you are fulfilling a certain sense of status, the absence of which had been troubling you for some time.

This is the worst possible approach you can take. You

are likely to end up owning a poorly-designed little box in a poorly-connected area, all the while saddled with a huge mortgage until beyond retirement. If you wish to avoid this fate, you need to find a way to *extract the emotion* out of home ownership—a difficult task admittedly, if you live in a country where *the Dream* and *the Property Ladder* are dogma.

If you are determined to wait for a significant drop in house prices before stepping in, you may well be on the right track. Just be vigilant and ensure that you are not simply a more patient version of the character described in the last paragraph. Explore whether your desire to buy "when the time is right" is driven by your own values and aspirations and not by what society or the people around you are making you believe. Thankfully, there is more to life than starring in an episode of *Grand Designs*.

There is also a third option, but it flies in the face of anglo-saxon property-owning dogma. If housing is an obsession and debt an addiction, then like with other drugs—just say no. It really is that simple.

And *you are allowed to do it*, regardless of what anyone says. Of course, as with drugs, there will be peer pressure to get you sucked into one of these schemes.

"But you must grow up and buy a home of your own some day. The government is helping you." Just say no.

"Paying rent is throwing money away. Buy a place now and you get to build equity of your own." Just say no.

"Don't you just love the pride of owning your own four walls?" Just say no.

"Are you not ashamed that your kids have to live in

rented accommodation?" Just say no.

Choose freedom, choose mobility, choose flexibility. If you are a young person with aspirations beyond thirty years of debt slavery, these three values will keep you one step ahead of the game. Despite what anyone tells you, you *can* rent a home for your entire life if you so choose, especially if the alternative is to subscribe to a scam like *Help to Buy*.

Be aware that you will inevitably upset a few people. By making a different lifestyle choice from friends, relatives and others around you, many will feel that you are tacitly (maybe even explicitly) criticizing their own choices. Perhaps they too could benefit from reading this book.

But none of the people you care about would benefit from you and your family being stuck for years on end in a cold little box that you can't sell, saddled with negative equity and monthly mortgage repayments which keep you trapped and prevent you from taking any new chances in life.

In times of uncertainty, it is natural to turn to others for advice. Beyond your friends and family, whom we just mentioned, be aware that your estate agent is not somebody to turn to for objective advice. Any day of the week, rain or shine, you can be certain to learn from your agent that "now is a great time to buy." And they will be especially thrilled to hear that with *Help to Buy*, you are now in a position to do so. Estate agents make their money from commission on the sales of homes. The greater the volume of transactions, the better. The higher the value of these transactions, the better. When prices take a fall, sales volumes tend to dry up. Estate agents much prefer steadily rising prices.

Likewise, the government stand to get voted out of power if a property market crash occurs on their watch. So their incentive is to keep things ticking higher for a bit longer, at least beyond the next election. They will never discourage you from wanting to buy; they will even emphasise that it is *your right*. Given the dynamics of the *Help to Buy* "equity loan" contract (in which the government participate in the upside or downside of the value of your home) they now have *even more of an incentive* to see ever-rising prices. An incentive which intensifies year by year of course, as more and more young people subscribe to *Help to Buy*!

As more and more young buyers are needed, with ever more "help" in order to buy at ever higher prices, it is starting to feel like a dangerous pyramid scheme. So please, be particularly vigilant towards financial advice from the government, including from the Money Advice Service (see www.moneyadviceservice.org.uk; "Free and impartial money advice, set up by the government").

Even your bank manager, who balks at the thought of lending you 95% of the property's value, is more relaxed about the prospect of lending you 75% or 80%. So long as you are making your monthly repayments, he could not care less whether you are able to afford the repayments comfortably, or merely scraping by from month to month. Even less so about your ability to sell and move house.

(For an example of a bank's very laid-back approach to your financial misfortunes, look no further than Santander, one of the UK's largest mortgage lenders. The company's helpful guide to the *Help to Buy* "equity loan" scheme (www.santanderforintermediaries.co.uk/downloads/1068) provides some easy-to-understand diagrams on page 2, which they have borrowed from H.M. Treasury. The third of these diagrams illustrates how much you would owe to the government (£36k in their example) in the event of a 10% fall in the value of your new home. But, carelessly, the bank doesn't take the trouble to emphasise the amount that you would also owe *them* (£150k in their example), nor the fact that the sum of these two debts (£186k) exceeds the value of the home (£180k). You would be in negative equity! But this is not made clear. Their guide does mention the risk of negative equity further down in a general sense, but the diagrams on page 2 only display the reduced amount owed to the government, giving the *distinct and misleading impression* that you are better off when prices have fallen. Whereas the opposite is true if you are leveraged up to your eyeballs!)

The point to take home here is not that all bankers are evil; it is that your banker is concerned only with your ability to repay the mortgage consistently, not with any sacrifices you may need to make in order to make those repayments, nor with the years of financial hardship your mortgage may subject you to. Like a tough boss who tells you "don't bring me excuses, just bring me results"... it's business.

These three groups—estate agents, the government and your mortgage lender—may indeed be "experts on the property market" in their respective fields, but you absolutely cannot count on them to offer you unbiased advice. Always ask yourself—and don't hesitate to ask them— "what happens if prices fall by 10% or more?". You may be in for a surprise.

If you remember just one thing, it should be this: They have no concern for your wellbeing. It's not that they hate you; they simply don't care.

There is nothing fundamentally wrong with owning a home, if that is what you genuinely want. There is however something deeply wrong about taking on excessive levels of debt in order to keep prices rising and to perpetuate somebody else's pyramid scheme.

CHAPTER SIX
After Sales: Damage Limitation

What will happen if you already have a huge mortgage (e.g. 95%) and especially if you have subscribed to a scheme like *Help to Buy*?

Your main risk is a fall in property prices—even a small one. If prices have risen since you bought your home, you are lucky to have a buffer against future price falls. There is nothing to stop you from selling up right now and simply "getting off the Property Ladder", having made a small profit (though do note that the government will confiscate their share of any profit you made, one of the conditions of *Help to Buy*).

Selling up before retirement would be utterly heretical behaviour of course, in total contradiction of the principles of *the Dream*, but you would get to cash in *and* reduce your risk—never a bad financial proposition if you can get it.

Besides, it's your life; you are free to choose your own dream.

If on the other hand you have only just recently bought a home with a large mortgage (greater than 80%), then you must start by acknowledging that you are highly vulnerable to any pullback in house prices. If you fall into negative equity, it doesn't mean that you automatically and immediately lose money, but it does mean that you are essentially trapped in that house or apartment until prices recover. Among other consequences, this may mean having to turn down new job opportunities and being unable to move to a different area for personal reasons.

Why would you be trapped? Let's imagine you bought your home last year for £300,000 with a £285,000 mortgage, but due to a fall in the property market, your house can now be sold for only £260,000. Even without accounting for any agency fees or removal costs, your £285,000 mortgage exceeds the proceeds of selling your home by £25,000. (£260k minus £285k equals -£25k.)

Whereas before, when the house was worth £300,000, you owned £15,000 in equity (this was your money; the white section in the illustration in Chapter 1), you are now stuck with £25,000 of leftover mortgage debt (negative equity). The bank still expects you to pay these £25,000 back somehow. You have personally lost £40,000 (£15k plus £25k)—that is everything you invested, *and more*. And you also no longer have a home to live in.

You may be forced to declare bankruptcy. You can certainly expect strains on your personal relationships and your health. Ouch.

For these painful reasons, most people simply hold off

The Help to Buy Scam

on selling unless forced to do so. But as a result, they end up trapped in that home. This could mean waiting for a year in the hope that prices recover, but it could mean waiting indefinitely. If you had bought a house in Japan in 1991, *you would still be waiting* for prices to recover to the level at which you bought. Don't fall into the same trap.

In the previous chapter, we mentioned the difficulties involved in turning to friends, family and property market experts for advice. Our advice is simple: If you are holding too much debt—and a 95% mortgage is too much debt—, you need to find a way to pay down that debt. In financial speak, you need to "de-leverage".

This is relatively simple but by no means easy. It means spending less on other items, such as cars, clothing, iPhones, travel, private schooling, Frappuccinos and everything else. If developing new sources of income is another option for you, then you should put this extra money towards paying back your mortgage at a faster rate than you are currently doing. We would recommend doing everything you realistically can in order to get your mortgage debt (including your "equity loan") below 80% of the value of your home.

You may be familiar with a paradox, known as the *Paradox of Thrift* (coined by J.M.Keynes), by which what is good for you as an individual saver is bad for the economy as a whole. Lower consumption, because of higher saving, leads to weaker economic growth.

Indeed, if you are a recent home owner on *Help to Buy*, "de-leveraging" is what *you* need to do, but it is not what the government, or your bank manager, want you to do. Partly because if everyone were to de-leverage, it would slow down the economy and lead to falling prices of goods and services (deflation), as has been happening in Japan for over 20 years.

Economic growth, in the form of increasing consumption and investment, has for the past few decades been fueled by excessive debt. Like in the run-up to 2008, we are now staring at a big bubble which may or may not burst in the coming few years. Oh, the suspense!

But let's be clear here: You personally did not get the world into this mess; you should have no qualms looking out for your own interests in this regard. Save yourself and your family and escape the trappings of excessive debt.

CONCLUSION

If you read the government's own assessments of *Help to Buy*, it has been a resounding success since its introduction in 2013. Indeed, in achieving its self-defined objective—namely, to allow 150,000 young people (and counting) to fulfill *the Dream*—it has succeeded magnificently.

But note the past tense. Mortgages last for decades. The government make little mention of the increased risks these young people now face, nor of the irresponsible manner in which they are being used in order to prop up a vulnerable housing market. Through market manipulation, the government can delay a fall in prices, but not prevent it altogether—as much as they would like to. When prices revert back to sensible levels (sooner or later, they always do) it is the financial situation of these young people that will be hit first and hit the hardest.

Call us alarmist if you wish, but you have been warned: *Help to Buy* and other such crackpot schemes are not here to help young people. They exist as an alternative to addressing the real estate bubble that has built up throughout the English-speaking world in particular, especially since the depths of the Global Financial Crisis in 2009. These schemes also act as a distraction from the demographic time bomb, in which Baby Boomers entering retirement hold insufficient pension assets to cover the costs of their old age.

Just as businesses listen to people who buy their products (or threaten not to), politicians listen to people who vote. Until young people begin to vote in greater numbers and demand better housing conditions, politicians will continue to sell them *the Dream* and to screw them over with such abusive schemes. In the meantime, the onus is on you to call "bullshit" and politely decline the government's so-called help.

ENDNOTES

---

[1] The Help to Buy mortgage guarantee is set to expire at the end of 2016.

[2] In mid 2016, interest rates are at historical lows. You also pay no interest on the "equity loan" for the first five years, after which you will pay a 1.75% "fee" (rising by the rate of inflation plus 1%). Which means that in 5 years' time, you may be facing significantly higher interest payments

[3] The Help to Buy: Equity Loan component of your debt does admittedly shield you slightly from the risk of price swings, certainly when compared to taking out additional mortgage debt. Indeed, the government shares some of the upside, and also some of the downside. But by boosting your spending power, the government is allowing you to buy an asset at an inflated cost, which is inherently risky.

www.ingramcontent.com/pod-product-compliance
Lightning Source LLC
Chambersburg PA
CBHW070421190526
45169CB00003B/1352